ثُنچارَن قيصةُ نبي عليهم السَّلام

Muhammad (pbuh) the Bearer of Islam

Abdul Rahman Rukaini

M
MACMILLAN PUBLISHERS

Bahasa Malay edition first published 1984.
Published by Macmillan Publishers (M) Sdn. Bhd. co-publication with
Pustaka Pertubuhan Kebajikan Islam Malaysia.

This edition first published 1985

Published by *Macmillan Publishers Ltd*
London and Basingstoke
Associated companies and representatives in Accra,
Auckland, Delhi, Dublin, Gaborone, Hamburg, Harare,
Hong Kong, Kuala Lumpur, Lagos, Manzini, Melbourne,
Mexico City, Nairobi, New York, Singapore, Tokyo.

ISBN 0−333−41426− 8(cased)
ISBN 0−333−40024− 0(pbk)

Printed in Hong Kong

Adviser for text:
Ustaz Haji Abu Hassan Din al-Hafiz

Adviser for illustrations:
Abdul Aziz Ibrahim

Designer and artist:
Abdul Razak Abdullah
(ERAL)

Illustrations found in these series were not meant to
depict all the prophets, their companions, or anyone
concerned during that time. These illustrations were
only meant to picture the situation or episodes that
happened during that time. The Publisher has
consulted authorised personnel to seek their advice
regarding the contents and illustrations.

British Library Cataloguing in Publication Data
Rukaini, Abdul Rahman
   Stories of the prophets of Islam.
   1. Prophets in the Koran—Biography—Juvenile
   literature
   I. Title
   297'.122'0922   BP134.P745

ISBN 0−333−41426− 8(cased)
ISBN 0−333−40024− 0(pbk)

Preface

Muhammad, as the last of the prophets of Islam, achieved what all the prophets before him had struggled to do; he ensured that the faith of Islam had triumphed and that it would be spread throughout the world by men and women for years to follow.

The stories in this volume tell us of Muhammad's escape from the leaders of the Quraysh; of the building of the mosque of the Prophet; of the brotherhood of Islam; and of the call to prayer. Finally we learn of Muhammad's triumph and of how his followers gathered in the field of Arafah to listen to his last sermon.

This is the last volume in the series *Stories of the Prophets of Islam*. All the stories have been based on episodes in the Quran and have shown how the great faith of the prophets enabled the spread of Islam.

The stories of their lives provide examples from which we can all learn.

Illustrations

Muhammad's hunters look for him in front of the cave. 6, 7.
Suraqah spurs his horse in search of Muhammad. 8, 9.
The people of Yathrib await Muhammad's arrival. 12, 13.
'Amr bin' Auf surveys the scene of the foundation of the first mosque. 15, 16, 17.
Muslims work together to build the first mosque. 18, 19.
A call to prayer. 24, 25.
Returning to Makkah. 26, 27.
Muslims gather at the field of Arafah in their Ihram costume. 28, 29.

Contents

An anxious moment

Abu Bakar's heart was beating so fast. He found it difficult to breathe. He knew that he and the Prophet were in great danger. Silently he prayed to Allah for protection.

The Prophet Muhammad sat silently by Abu Bakar's side. They were hiding in a cave in the mountains of Thur and their enemies were searching for them. But still the Prophet was calm and unafraid.

When the leaders of the Quraysh found they had been tricked and Muhammad had managed to escape from Makkah without being seen, they set out to look for him. Groups of men went off in different directions.

One group, led by a man who was clever at following tracks arrived at the bottom of the mountain of Thur. Their eyes searched the mountain-side, looking for signs of Abu Bakar and the Prophet. Abu Bakar could see them from his hiding place in the mouth of the cave. The hunters were talking to a goatherd and looking up towards the cave. Abu Bakar was so afraid they would climb the mountain and find the cave where he and the Prophet were hidden.

'It doesn't look easy to climb', said one of the hunters. 'It's so steep and there are no foot-holds.' The man was tired. He wanted to give up the search. He and his friends had been promised a hundred camels by the leaders of the Quraysh if they found Muhammad. He didn't think it was worth risking his life on the steep mountain–side for a hundred camels. But his friends did, and they carried on. They didn't know whether Muhammad was right or not, and they did not care. They knew the leaders of the Quraysh were always attacking Muhammad, and they were being paid good money to find him.

6

One of them was a good climber. Soon he was near the top of the mountain. Muhammad and Abu Bakar knew the man was near. Abu Bakar held his breath but the Prophet calmly recited the words of the Quran:

'Remember when the unbelievers plotted against you to kill you or send you into exile. They tried to trick Allah but Allah will repay them, as He does all who lie and cheat.' (*Al Quran, Surah al-Anfal, verse 30*)

The words calmed Abu Bakar for a moment, but then he saw the climber right at the mouth of the cave! The man's hands were scratched and bleeding from his climb. He was

looking at his hands, then something caught his attention. It was a spider in the centre of its web. The web hung right across the entrance to the cave. And on a hollow in the rock, a dove had made her nest. The man looked closer. The bird was sitting on her eggs.

The man was sure no one had gone into the cave through this entrance. The dove and the spider had clearly been there a long time. He began to walk round to look for another way into the cave.

Abu Bakar's heart leapt. Only Allah could save them. Allah had made the spider and the dove appear. But now the man was standing right by another entrance to the cave. Abu Bakar moved closer to the Prophet.

'If he bends down, he'll see us', he whispered. Muhammad knew his friend was afraid and recited these words from the Quran:

'If you do not help him, Allah will help him, as He helped him when he and another were driven out by the non-believers. Then in the cave when he said to his friend, "Do not be afraid. Allah is with us" Allah strengthened his spirit and sent to his aid unseen helpers. Allah is mighty and wise.' (*Al Quran, at-Taubah, verse 40*)

Abu Bakar stopped feeling afraid. The man outside the cave did not bend down. He shouted down to his friends below to continue their search for the Prophet elsewhere.

One hundred camels

After four days of hiding in the cave, Muhammad's faithful servant came to him secretly, as they had arranged. He brought camels for them to ride and the little party set off for Yathrib. They were still afraid of being followed, so they went west towards the coast then turned north.

At midday they stopped in the shade of a rock and managed to buy some milk from a passing goatherd. After a rest they went on.

News of the reward offered for finding Muhammad spread throughout the country. When Suraqah heard from the goatherd about the people he had seen near the coast, Suraqah was sure it was the Prophet and his companions. He told the other people in his village that Muhammad had been seen nearby and sent them off to look for him. But Suraqah was clever. He wanted the reward for himself, so he sent the others in the wrong direction. Then, when he was sure no one could see him, he saddled his horse and rode towards the place where the goatherd had met the travellers.

Suraqah spurred his horse on fiercely. He ignored the blistering heat of the sun on his face. He was determined to capture Muhammad.

'Faster! Faster!' he cried. His heart pounded like the horse's hoof beats. He smiled as he thought of the reward of one hundred camels.

But suddenly his horse stumbled. Suraqah lost the reins as his horse fell. Suraqah was thrown headlong into the sand. He picked himself up and his horse struggled to its feet. Suraqah stroked his horse then got back on and galloped even faster along the shore of the Red Sea, the wind in his face. But his horse fell again, and Suraqah was thrown off again.

Again he got back on and galloped in the direction of the plains of Tuhamah. That was where the goat-herd had told him the travellers were heading.

His eyes searched the grasslands ahead for a sign of the party. His heart raced. He knew the Prophet was not alone. He would probably have to kill or be killed.

Abu Bakar heard the beat of the horse's hooves and looked round. His voice shook with fear as he told the Prophet they were being followed. Calmly the Prophet told him, 'Do not be afraid. Allah is with us.'

As they prayed, Suraqah's horse began to sink into the sand. Suraqah's bravery disappeared. He began to scream for help. The

Prophet and his companions turned back.

'By Allah, have pity on me', cried Suraqah. He and his horse were still sinking into the sand.

'Why did you come here?' asked Muhammad.

'I was paid. There is a reward of a hundred camels for your capture. Forgive me', cried the unhappy Suraqah. He promised to give everything he had to the Prophet.

'If you are an enemy of Islam, your gifts mean nothing to me', said Muhammad.

Suraqah's eyes were round with fear.

'I will do whatever you want, sir', he promised.

'Then you must stop anyone from coming after us', said the Prophet.

Suraqah nodded. 'I know your religion will triumph in the world. You will be the Prophet of mankind', he cried.

The Prophet prayed, 'O Allah! If his words are true, release him and his horse.'

Immediately the horse sprang to his feet. Suraqah knelt to pray to the Prophet in thanks. Then he got on his horse and galloped home a wiser man.

Waiting

For years the people in the country around Yathrib had been at war. But at last they had heard of a man who could lead them and bring peace and now they were waiting to welcome the Prophet. They had heard that he had left Makkah, 300 miles away, and was on his way to their city. They knew it was a difficult journey and prayed to Allah as they waited on the outskirts of the city, to let the Prophet arrive safely.

News had reached them that the Prophet had left the mountain of Thur, then that he had arrived at Tuhamah. They heard that Suraqah had chased the travellers but Allah had saved them. In the towns and villages the people showed their joy at the Prophet's escape.

'The Prophet is coming here. He will be our guest!' they cried. Everyone made preparations to celebrate the Prophet's arrival. Everyone hoped that the Prophet would be his guest.

The Prophet's followers wanted to show their loyalty to him.

'This is not a pilgrimage festival', said 'Uqbah. They all listened to him: his own people, the leaders of the other tribes, and their people, the Muslims, who had already arrived from Makkah.

'This is the time to show the loyalty we promised to the Prophet', said 'Uqbah. 'We must give our lives, our time and our money to fight for the Prophet's cause. Friends, will you leave your fields and your businesses to welcome the Prophet?'

Their cries drowned 'Uqbah's voice.

'We will wait at the walls of the city! We will wait with the spirit of unity and brotherhood!'

Soon the streets of the city of Yathrib were lined with people. Some people waited on the city walls, some waited outside the city, in nearby Quba'. The morning passed, then the afternoon. Evening came, and night. Still the Prophet had not arrived. The people began to worry.

'The Prophet will come', said 'Uqbah. He tried to reassure himself and the other people waiting with him.

'When?'

'Tomorrow. The day after. It doesn't matter when he comes. We'll wait for him.'

'I hope no one's trying to stop him from getting here', said someone in the crowd.

In his heart 'Uqbah thought there must be something wrong. Or maybe the Prophet had stopped to rest somewhere? 'Uqbah knew the leaders of Makkah had failed to stop the Prophet. They had just added to their sins with their attempts to catch him.

'He must have stopped for the night', thought 'Uqbah to himself. 'But I will go on waiting because I know he will arrive at last!'

A young man called out. Everyone turned in his direction. Had Muhammad arrived? 'Uqbah ran up to him.

'Yes, Muhammad will be here soon', said the young man. The Prophet had arrived at Quba', only two miles away.

'My friends, you must not worry', cried 'Uqbah happily. 'Muhammad has arrived in Quba'!' he shouted to the crowd. Hearing the good news, the people waited with renewed excitement.

The mosque

That night was unlike other nights. Everyone in the valley felt that it was special. It was the 13th night of Rabiulawal. The full moon shone from the sky. The moonlight touched the trees and the earth, and 'Amr's house. It was a magical night.

'Amr was walking back to his house. He was returning from the new mosque of Quba'. The Prophet Muhammad had laid the foundation stone that day. 'Amr turned round to look at the mosque again. He smiled. 'This is the gift of Allah', he said to himself. Allah had saved the people of Yathrib and the people of Quba' from ignorance.

'Amr looked up at the moon. The light of the moon shone in his eyes. He remembered how people had once worshipped the moon because of its light. 'Amr knew the message of the Prophet was brighter than moonlight. He felt that the light of

14

Islam was inside him. He was a true believer. Truth would triumph over evil.

'This mosque is the symbol of righteousness', 'Amr thought to himself. He remembered the words from the Quran:

'It is in the mosque built from the beginning on a foundation of righteousness that you should worship. In that mosque you will find men who keep pure. Allah will love those who purify themselves.' (*Al Quran, Surah At-Taubah, verse 108*)

It was these words that had made 'Amr want to go and look at the foundation stones of the new Quba' mosque in the moonlight. He knew that the mosque was a symbol of the greatness of Islam, the people of Islam and the nation of Islam. If the mosque was a failure, it would mean that Islam no longer shone, that the light of the moon was dimmed. The people of Islam would become weaker and fewer too.

'I will guard this mosque', thought 'Amr to himself, 'as faithfully as the Prophet has guarded his people.'

He turned back towards his home and walked on firmly. He knew that the religion which had been persecuted in Makkah was growing in Yathrib. The Prophet would have been killed in Makkah, but in Yathrib he was free and loved. The name of the city had now been changed to Medinaten Nabi (City of the Prophet) in honour of the Prophet's arrival. (The name was soon shortened to Medina.)

'Allah will always protect us. In the end we will triumph', thought 'Amr as he walked home proudly. He wanted to tell all the Arabs in Makkah that the Prophet was sleeping safely under his, 'Amr's, roof. His joy at receiving such an honoured guest shone in his eyes. He thought of Abu Jahal who had lead the people of Makkah against the Prophet.

'You thought Islam could be defeated by force, but you were wrong', he said aloud, as if he were face to face with the cruel Abu Jahal.

'Amr went quietly into his house. The Prophet and Abu Bakar were sleeping peacefully. They were exhausted from their long and difficult journey. 'Amr lay down on his bed, but he could not sleep. He was so overjoyed to be the host of these honoured guests. He sat up and opened the window. Moonlight poured in, with a cooling breeze. Next day people would gather at 'Amr's house to meet the Prophet. Together they would complete the building of the mosque of Quba', the symbol of the strength of Islam.

'Amr lay down again and moved his lips in a prayer. Then he closed his eyes and fell into a peaceful sleep.

بسم الله الرحمن الرحيم

The road to Heaven

It was a beautiful clear day. A gentle, fresh wind blew small white clouds across the sky. The sun was warm but not too hot. The people who had gathered on the patch of bare land were happy and joking with each other.

The Prophet Muhammad and Abu Bakar were there, together with the Muhajirin (the Prophet's followers who had come to Medina to be with him) and the Ansar (the Prophet's supporters in Medina).

Sahal was the happiest of all of

them. He smiled to himself as he looked round the clearing.

'All the trees I planted have been cut down', he said to himself with a smile. He didn't mind. Yesterday he had worked from dawn to dusk with his friends to clear the land. This was the spot where Muhammad's camel had stopped when the Prophet entered Medina. Sahal owned the

land, which was covered in date-palms, but willingly he had given the land as the site for a mosque.

'I would do anything for the faith!' he was thinking to himself when a voice interrupted his thoughts.

'May Allah repay you well.' Sahal turned to see his friend, who clasped Sahal's hand and embraced him.

'You have set foot on the road', said the friend. Sahal smiled. He knew what his friend meant: the road to Heaven.

'It was Allah who showed me the way', said Sahal, freeing himself from his friend's embrace. He remembered what he had said to the Prophet. 'We do not prize our gardens and fruit trees, except in the service of Allah. Everything is Allah's.'

Sahal and his friend remembered the words of the Quran which they had heard:

'The goods which are spent on the road to Allah are like seeds. Each seed sprouts seven shoots and each shoot bears a hundred fruits . . .'

This was Allah's promise. This was the belief of Sahal and every man of the faith.

'Someone who provides the land for a mosque is paving the road to Heaven for himself and others', said Sahal's friend.

'And the same is true of someone who helps to build a mosque', added Sahal.

A lot of people had gathered ready to start work. Sahal watched the Prophet lift the first stone and set it down in its place. He was followed by Abu Bakar. Everyone watched. Then Umar, Uthman and Ali each laid a stone.

The Prophet looked at the people gathered round him. 'They will be the Khalifs of Islam after me', he said when Ali had laid the fifth stone.

Everyone set to work happily. They all worked hard. The Prophet worked with them. He sang as he worked:

'Oh Allah! Truly our reward is only in the world beyond.
Give Your blessing to the Ansar and Muhajirin.
Free them from the burning torture of Hell,
For that fire is only for the evil and the unbelievers.'

The Prophet's friends listened to the words of the song as they worked. Then they sang together:

'We will not sit idle while the Prophet rests.

That would be a sign that we are lost.'

Then their voices were joined by the voices of the Muhajirin and the Ansar in a hymn of praise:

'O Allah! There is no life but in the next life.
Give the flower of Your blessing to the Muhajirin and the Ansar.
O Allah! There is no worth but in the next life.
Give the flower of Your blessing to the Muhajirin and the Ansar.'

The voices of the Prophet and his friends rose in harmony, like the waves of the sea, like a heavenly choir of angels.

Sahal and his friend added their voices as they joined in the hymn. They did not notice the weight of the stones they lifted or the beams of wood they carried over their shoulders. All their feelings were absorbed in the rhythm and flow of the sacred hymn. The walls of the mosque grew higher. Soon the shape of the building was quite clear.

'Well, Sahal?' said his friend, wondering why Sahal was smiling to himself.

Sahal turned to his friend who was working beside him. 'It's wonderful, wonderful', he said. His friend understood his joy. It lay in a plot of land, a building of stones, logs and palm leaves. The joy was spread by the voice of the muezzin and all the builders of the mosque.

Only the faithful are brothers

It was five months since the pilgrims had arrived in Medina. It was five months since they had left their homeland, their villages, their palm trees, their camels, their sheep, their families, and everything they owned. For Allah and His Prophet they had left everything they loved most. They had fought and risked their lives for them. All they hoped for was the blessing of Allah.

But not everyone in Medina supported the Prophet. The Jews were still his enemy, and there were the people called the Munafiks. These people pretended to become Muslims but they did not really believe and they plotted against the Prophet and his followers.

The Munafiks were hoping to divide Muhammad's followers, to turn the Ansar against the Muhajirin.

'We will say that the Muhajirin have brought nothing but problems to Medina', said one of the Munafiks. The Muhajirin were poor because even those who had been wealthy had had to leave everything behind when they followed the Prophet to Medina. The Munafiks

thought they could make the Ansar resent sharing their homes and food with the Muhajirin. They thought they could make Muslim hate Muslim.

The Prophet Muhammad heard of the plans of the Munafiks. He had known from the beginning that they had not accepted Islam sincerely. They spoke the words of the faith but in their hearts they did not believe. The Prophet wanted to strengthen the friendship between the Muhajirin and the Ansar, to form a brotherhood of Islam. He discussed his idea with Abu Bakar and Umar and a decision was made.

Abu Bakar, Umar, Ali and Uthman called all the Muhajirin and Ansar to the mosque. They waited to hear the Prophet's words.

'. . . We must be bound in brotherhood', said the Prophet. He held Ali's hand up. 'This is my brother!' he cried. 'Hamzah is the brother of Zaid bin Harithah . . .'

The people understood. Each member of the Muhajirin would swear brotherhood with a member of the Ansar. Only people of the faith were brothers. The Munafiks and the non-believers were not brothers. They were all enemies of the religion of Allah and His Prophet.

The Muhajirin and Ansar swore brotherhood in pairs. Then their brotherly love was shown by the help which each Ansar offered his Muhajirin brother, who owned nothing. This help was offered for love of Allah.

S'ad wanted to give part of his house and his orchards to Abdul Rahman. 'Brother,' he said, 'take all this.'

Abdul Rahman smiled. He knew his 'brother' was sincere. He was touched by his kindness but he could not accept such a gift.

'Thank you', he said, embracing S'ad. 'May Allah bless you, your family and everything you own. But I cannot take such a gift from you. Just show me a place in the market where I can trade then I will have all I need.'

S'ad understood and did all he could to help Abdul Rahman. All the other brothers helped each other too.

The Munafiks heard about the brotherhood. They were angry. They had not been included, and their plans had been ruined.

'This brotherhood will isolate us', said one of the Munafiks.

'You're right', said another. 'This means unity and strength for Islam.'

They did not like to think of the Muslims triumphing.

'The Prophet must have found out about our plan', said another gloomily. He knew how wise the Prophet was.

'I think so, too. Muhammad plans to strengthen the unity of his followers and to exclude us.'

The brotherhood was a blow to the Munafiks, but they did not tell the Jews. The Jews had promised them a lot of money to destroy the Muslims. The Munafiks still tried to divide the people of the faith, but they failed. The Muslims were stronger than ever. For the Muhajirin and the Ansar, the fight for Islam was just beginning.

بِسْمِ اللهِ الرَّحْمَنِ الرَّحِيمِ

The call to prayer

At dusk the voice rang out through the clear evening air. '*Al-salatu jami'ah. Al-salatu jami'ah!*' The same man, the same voice, called every night at the same time.

The beauty of the voice affected everyone who heard it. They found their feet drawn towards the Mosque of the Prophet. The sacred sounds filled their hearts. Even the wind, the birds and the trees seemed to bow down before the sound of that voice. Only the heart of a devil could resist it!

All the Muhajirin and Ansar rose when they heard the call and began to make their way to the mosque of the Prophet. Abdullah bin Zaid was amongst them. The words meant something very special to him. He

had heard them in a dream one night.

A man in a green robe had appeared before him, when he was lying in bed. The man had a bell in his hand and Abdullah had asked him, 'Do you want to sell your bell?'

'What do you want it for?' the man had asked.

'To call the people to prayer.'

'I can give you something better', replied the man. 'Call them with these words.'

Now as he walked, Abdullah remembered the words of the Prophet Muhammad when he had told him about the dream. 'That dream was a true vision', Muhammad had said.

Abdullah knew the words were

important not just to him, but to all Muslims. He walked on, listening to the beautiful voice.

'Allah is the Greatest! Allah is the Greatest!' Abdullah felt very small compared to the greatness of Allah.

'I bear witness that there is none worthy of worship except Allah!' the voice rang out.

Abdullah's lips moved in prayer as he walked towards the mosque. He reached the entrance as the first stage of the call to prayer ended.

The meaning of the prayer flowed in Abdullah's veins. He lived only to serve the true religion.

'I bear witness that Muhammad is a messenger of Allah!
Let us worship!
Let us seek blessedness!'

The words made Abdullah weep with joy. He repeated the sacred words,

'Allah is the Greatest! There is none worthy of worship except Allah!'

His face was calm. He knelt and lifted his hands as he prayed:

'This is a true and righteous prayer. This is the tribute which You have required. You sent to us the worthy Prophet. You have bestowed on him the greatest honour.'

Abdullah went into the mosque. He wanted to worship on his own, in the strength of his faith, before the muezzin gave the call for the evening worship.

The return to Makkah

The people of Makkah and their leaders, Abu Sufyan, Budail and Hakim had broken their treaty with the Muslims of Medina. Now Muhammad and his followers had a reason to attack Makkah. The struggle between the people of Medina and the people of Makkah had continued, even after the battle of Badr. But that war had marked the beginning of the great period of Islam. Even Abu Sufyan, Budail and Hakim had to admit that the Prophet had triumphed and they had failed.

'What will happen if the Muslims attack Makkah?' thought Abu Sufyan to himself. Anxiously he and his two companions looked out from their hiding place in the hill at Mara-al-Zahran.

'Look at that huge fire over there!' cried Hakim, pointing into the darkness.

'It's so big, it must be a company of soldiers!'

'It's probably the Khuza'ah tribe', said Budail, trying not to be frightened.

'The Khuza'ah? They are only a small tribe. This is a huge fire', said Abu Sufyan. Each of them thought of the Prophet and his troops. They were afraid and didn't know what to do.

Their words had been overheard by Abbas, the uncle of the Prophet. They had not seem him come to their hiding place. His voice broke the silence of the night.

'Abu Sufyan', he said. They started. Abu Sufyan recognised the voice.

'Is that you, Abbas?' he asked. 'What are you doing here?'

'Abu Sufyan, in the name of Allah

'I ask you to look over there', said Abbas, pointing to the fire in the distance. 'Over there is the army of the Prophet Muhammad. They are approaching Makkah . . . if they attack, Makkah will be destroyed.'

Abu Sufyan was silent. He knew Abbas was right.

'If you oppose the Prophet and you are caught, you will be killed', added Abbas. He told Abu Sufyan that the only thing he could do was to surrender himself to the Prophet and ask for his protection.

'Yes, I agree', said Abu Sufyan weakly. He mounted a white donkey with Abbas and rode into the darkness. The Prophet had sent Abbas on his own donkey to fetch Abu Sufyan.

When Umar heard that Abu Sufyan had arrived in the Prophet's camp he came to see the Prophet.

'Now we have caught Abu Sufyan, let me cut off his head', demanded Umar. But Abbas refused.

'I brought him here and I guaranteed his safety', Abbas replied.

The Prophet was silent. Then he turned to Abu Sufyan and asked him to accept Islam, to confess that there was only one God, Allah, and to admit that Muhammad was His prophet. Abu Sufyan was reluctant. But he could see he had no choice. At last he agreed. Now the Prophet and his followers could return to Makkah in peace.

From Makkah they came, and to Makkah they returned. The truth had triumphed! Makkah and Medina became the centres of Islam.

The power of prayer

Like the dawn over any desert, the dawn at Mina was clear and beautiful. The sun shed its light over the hills. The sun's rays were gentle. They seemed to respect the place where the Prophet and his 14,000 followers had recently camped.

It was the morning of 9th Zulhijjah. The Prophet and his followers had arrived late on the

night of 8th Zulhijjah. They left Makkah, where they had stayed since 4th Zulhijjah, in the early evening. They had just finished performing the fifth pillar of Islam, the Haj. This was the grandest pilgrimmage since 25th Zulhijjah, 10 Hijarah.

This morning, as the Prophet Muhammad rode his camel towards Arafah, twenty-two years of bitterness and hardship in the spread of Islam had ended. The whole population of the Arab peninsula had accepted Islam. Evil had been destroyed. Truth triumphed. The Arabs had freed themselves from ignorance and followed the true religion. The Jews and the other non-believers left the Arabs alone, to serve Allah.

The journey to Arafah was peaceful. There was silence except for voices raised in the Talbiyah, a verse praising God. The powerful words had echoed from Medina, Zulhulafah and Makkah. 14,000 voices recited the holy verse. The

words calmed them, strengthened their faith. The valleys rang with the voices of the faithful, all the way to Arafah.

'O Allah! Your servant answers Your call to serve You. You are one. There is none other than You. All praise to You, for the success that has come to us is Yours. Your servant comes to serve You.'

In the fields at the foothills the pilgrims gathered together. They were all dressed in white clothing. 14,000 people welcomed Muhammad as he arrived from Namirah, a village to the east of Arafah.

It was here, under the setting sun, that Muhammad gave his sermon. It was to be his last sermon, but none of his followers knew that. They stood in silence in the burning heat, anxious to hear his words.

'All praise is to God. I bear witness that there is no God other than Allah the Mighty. You are One. There is none other than You. I bear witness that Muhammad is Your servant and prophet.'

All eyes were on the Prophet as he spoke to his followers.

'You and your belongings will be respected, as is this day and this month. When you appear before your Lord, He will ask what good you have done. Do not be led astray when I am gone.'

In his sermon, Muhammad spoke of the women, '. . . You have a duty to your wives, as they have to you. I ask you to give good guidance to the women. They can help you.'

Muhammad ended his sermon with these words:

'I leave you the Holy Book, the Quran. If you keep to it, you will not be led astray.

'Have I fulfilled my responsibilities?' With one voice, the 14,000 followers of the Prophet cried out, 'In the name of Allah, yes.'

Calmly Muhammad answered, 'Bear witness, O Allah.'

How proud they were listening to the Prophet's sermon. And how happy they were to see such a huge congregation. But there were a few of his companions who were puzzled by these words of the Prophet:

'Please listen to me. I do not know whether I will meet with you at this same place again . . .'

Whatever Muhammad meant by this, the words of Allah were brought down in the last verse of the Asar prayer in Arafah. Islam has triumphed and spread throughout the world.